SWEET TREATS
FROM THE
WILD WEST

Chase Reynolds Ewald
Amy Jo Sheppard

GIBBS·SMITH
➜P
PUBLISHER

Salt Lake City

For Charles and his girls, dedicated cookie-eaters.
C.R.E.

And for Grandma Schneider and Grandma Sheppard and Mom—
they are why I love to be in the kitchen.
A.J.S.

First Edition
03 02 01 00 99   5 4 3 2 1

Text copyright © 1999
    by Chase Reynolds Ewald and Amy Jo Sheppard
Photographs copyright © 1999
    by Gibbs Smith, Publisher

Published by
Gibbs Smith, Publisher
P.O. Box 667
Layton, Utah 84041

Orders: (1-800) 748-5439
E-mail: info@gibbs-smith.com

Photography by Elijah Cobb, Cody, Wyoming
Book design by Trent Alvey Design
Printed and bound in Malaysia

Library of Congress Cataloging-in-Publication Data

Ewald, Chase Reynolds, 1963–
    Sweet treats from the wild west / Chase Reynolds
Ewald, Amy Jo Sheppard.
        p.   cm.
    ISBN 0-87905-917-6
    1. Desserts. 2. Cookery—Rocky Mountain Region.
I. Sheppard, Amy Jo, 1965– . II. Title.
TX773.E834   1999
641.8'6—dc21   99-27332
                                                 CIP

Contents

Foreword

One of the enduring memories from my childhood is of the desserts my mother cooked when we lived on a ranch in New Mexico in the early 1950s. Mom was a whiz at cakes and candy (her fudge and divinity are to die for), not to mention Swedish tea rings full of raisins, nuts, and cinnamon and lightly glazed with white frosting. In true ranch style, she often decorated her pies with local cattle brands made from strips of dough laid over the pie filling.

Living thirty miles from town, miles from the nearest neighbor and with no telephone, Mom was as resourceful as any chuck wagon cook and a whole lot easier to get along with. I never recall her referring to a cookbook, though she may have once in a while. She was a quick study in the kitchen, working from taste and texture until each dish was just right.

More than forty years have passed since our family moved from the ranch to town and even longer since roundup cooks with names like "Whistling Jake" served sweet treats like "son-of-a-gun-in-a-sack" and "spotted pup" from a Dutch oven.

The recipes in this volume are a far cry from the days when butter, milk, and eggs were in short supply in the West and when preparing dessert meant stewing dried fruit in a kettle or pouring "lick" (molasses) from a can. Today's western cooks have more ingredients and options than ever. Add a little imagination and adventurous spirit to the delicious recipes on the pages that follow and introduce your taste buds to a new frontier.

B. Byron Price
Executive Director, Buffalo Bill Historical Center

Introduction

We were lucky enough to come together at Breteche Creek, a 7,000-acre cattle ranch in a dramatic mountain setting halfway between Yellowstone Park and Cody. Chase had started a nonprofit foundation operating out of a remote valley on Bo and Anna Polk's ranch in 1991. Amy Jo came on board as chef for the summer guest program in 1995. It was soon apparent that her people skills outshone even her culinary skills, and before the summer was out, she had become director of Breteche Creek Foundation. We were united by our twin passions: the wild parts of the American West and creative, fresh, well-prepared food. The two haven't always been paired in the same sentence, however, and we both felt we could work toward changing that.

Breteche Creek operates akin to a traditional dude ranch to offer guests the opportunity to master horseback riding and the fine art of "pushing cows" in the rugged, mountainous Yellowstone country. What makes Breteche Creek different (other than the superlative food) is that we also offer education in natural history and regional culture. We discuss holistic range management while herding cattle, and practice horsemanship with one of the finest horse trainers in the region. We learn geology from high atop a mountain and hear from an astronomer about the stars while viewing them under a brilliant night sky. An archaeologist may teach about the Plains Indians who lived in our valley and demonstrate how to make arrowheads. A wildlife biologist might lecture on grizzly bears and show budding naturalists how to distinguish their tracks. Drawing, painting, photography, and nature writing are practiced outdoors in a valley surrounded by mountains and fringed with lodgepole pines and quaking aspens.

At Breteche Creek our lives have been enriched by the many wonderful guests who've come to us from all over the world. We've learned much from them and they from us, and more importantly, from the natural world. We've made many lasting friendships, for which we are deeply grateful. Virtually all our guests who arrive expecting meat and 'taters have been impressed by the food they've been served. Many have suggested we produce a cookbook based on our approach to western cuisine. We chose desserts first because we love 'em, and, besides, we both bake a mean cookie.

The recipes are original, having evolved from classic recipes, or because something we saw or read or sampled gave us a new idea. Sometimes the ideas have arrived in our minds fully conceived, as if a houseguest arrived on our doorstep bearing his own artfully prepared meals, ready to share. We've been lucky to include recipes from ten of our favorite restaurants around the Rockies, and these are truly expressions of the New West—a region (and some say state of mind) that looks fondly back while embracing the future.

In the historic West, recipes came from indigenous cultures as well as from the homelands of the settlers: New England, the South, the Southwest, Europe, Scandinavia, China, and Mexico. The West, as much as anyplace else in America, was truly a melting pot. Recipes took on regional flavor when adapted with ingredients at hand. Today we continue that tradition by drawing on a heritage from France to Mexico, and not being afraid to occasionally employ such exotic imports as macadamia nuts and coconut. Pioneer women were experts at making do with what was in their larders. Although we embrace modern refrigeration and transportation systems that allow us to have fresh produce and unusual ingredients year-round, we would never "run to the store" for just one ingredient. It's wasteful and usually unnecessary.

A word on calories: Cowboys never worried about their figures. As far as they were concerned, the sweeter the better. Fat was simply not an issue. Although we believe cookies, not people, should be round, we also believe that if you're going to do something, you might as well do it right. Thus, unless a severe dietary restriction must be taken into account, we use butter, not margarine; whole eggs, not egg substitutes. When it comes to eating, we believe in moderation. (Luckily, we also love to ride, hike, ski, and mountain bike.)

In gratitude for the mountains we love and the foundation that brought us together, we're devoting a percentage of the proceeds from this book to Breteche Creek Foundation. Funds will be used to help the important work of exposing people to what's most special and most threatened in the American West, and in supporting such goals as holistic range management. For more information, contact Breteche Creek Foundation at P.O. Box 596, Cody, Wyoming 82414, phone (307) 587-3844, or E-mail breteche@wavecom.net. For those who can't live in the West, who haven't bonded with a horse, flushed an elk, identified bear-claw marks, confronted a rattlesnake, admired western wildflowers, or pushed cows at a slow walk while smelling the sagebrush under an impossibly broad sky of cloudless blue—well, we hope this book brings a little slice of our West into your home.

Chase Reynolds Ewald and Amy Jo Sheppard

Acknowledgments

This book was definitely a group effort. We'd like to acknowledge the best of the New West: the chefs of The Gallatin Gateway Inn, Gallatin Gateway, Montana; La Comida, Cody, Wyoming; Log Haven, Salt Lake City; Maxwell's, Cody; The Range, Jackson Hole; Skyline Ranch, Telluride; The Snake River Grill, Jackson Hole; Spanish Peaks Brewery, Bozeman; The Park Cafe, St. Mary, Montana; and The Sun Valley Lodge.

A big "thank you" is due our agent, Diana Finch, our editor, Madge Baird, photographer Elijah Cobb, and photo stylist Anne Smith; all helped make this a great book. Thanks to Bo and Anna Polk for so much more than a test kitchen; to Dede Johnson; to our testing panel: Deb Hayber, Kathryn Hiestand, Kristy Bradford Hoffman, Shannon Gormley and Scott Nelson, Deborah Minor, Debbie Reynolds, Melissa Scott, Hannah Sweet, and Elise Thompson. We couldn't have done the photo shoot without help from Robin Caddy, Sue Simpson Gallagher, Deb Hayber, Julie Kenney, Joel Nields, Linda Raynolds, Kerry Strike, Debra Reilly of The Thistle, Ev and Sue Diehl of Cody Rodeo Company, and Cody craftsmen Jim Covert, John Gallis, and Mike Patrick.

Finally, we'd like to pay tribute to our mothers, for teaching us to bake our first cookies; to Addie and Jessie, for making sure the bowls were clean; to Vone, Flor, and Nanon, for everything; to Charles, for agreeing to eat cookies instead of dinner; and to Melissa, for putting up with chaos in her Bozeman kitchen.

Cowboy Cookies

The great melting pot that it is, America has had little in the form of a truly indigenous cuisine. The hamburger? Perhaps. Apple pie? Sure. Cookies? Definitely!

Cookies, like the cowboy, are a uniquely American expression, having sprung from our culture fully formed and with a decidedly American accent. Like that other American standby, sandwiches, there is no end to what can be put in a cookie. Cookies are practical: they can be frozen whole, frozen as dough, or baked and kept for several days. And they can stand up to rough treatment in the saddlebag. Cookies are about the only thing a child will never say no to. Most important, though, is the sheer satisfaction they pack. After all, there are few taste sensations more luxurious than biting into a warm cookie with chewy, slightly crunchy edges and molten chocolate chips.

Cookies make wonderful gifts, too, at holiday time or as an alternative to the de rigeur bottle of wine one brings to supper at a friend's house. They're appropriate at most any time of the day. And, although they may have attitude, they're never pretentious.

We've included our own versions of wonderful old standbys, including pecan sandies, molasses chews, and old-fashioned peanut-butter cookies. We've expanded the range of traditional flavors with ingredients such as crystallized ginger, almond butter, dried cherries, and pine nuts. We've broadened the western horizons with such internationally influenced recipes as biscotti, and thrown in more contemporary, health-conscious ingredients such as wheat germ. Cookies—they're not just for children anymore.

Cowpoke Cranberry-Coconut Cookies

These are delicious and different—a great treat for the cowpokes in your corral.

1/2 cup butter
1/2 cup shortening
3/4 cup sugar
3/4 cup brown sugar
2 eggs
2 teaspoons vanilla
1 teaspoon baking soda
1/2 teaspoon salt
1-1/2 cups white flour
3/4 cup whole-wheat flour
1 cup pecans, coarsely chopped
    and toasted
1 cup coconut flakes, lightly toasted
3/4 cup dried cranberries

Preheat oven to 350 degrees. Cream butter, shortening, and sugars together. Beat in eggs and vanilla. Mix baking soda, salt, and flours together and stir into wet ingredients until just combined. Stir in pecans, coconut, and cranberries. Form into 1" balls and place on ungreased cookie sheet about 2" apart. Bake in oven 10 to 15 minutes, until cookies start to brown on top.

Chocolate Ginger Chocolate-Chip Cookies

A decadent treat with a flavorful zing. (If the ginger is too intense, cut the amount by half.)

2/3 cup butter
1 cup sugar
1 egg
1-1/2 cups white flour
1/3 cup cocoa
1/4 teaspoon salt
1/4 teaspoon baking powder
1/4 teaspoon baking soda
3/4 cup crystallized ginger, chopped
1 cup pecans, chopped and toasted
6 ounces semisweet chocolate chips

Preheat oven to 350 degrees. Cream butter and sugar. Beat in egg. Stir in flour, cocoa, salt, baking powder, and baking soda. Stir in ginger, pecans, and chocolate chips. Roll dough into 1-1/2" balls. Roll balls in sugar. Place about 3" apart on ungreased cookie sheet. Flatten with the bottom of a glass. Bake until cookies crinkle on top and are slightly set, about 9 minutes.

Center: Chocolate Ginger Chocolate-Chip; clockwise from bottom: Wild Huckleberry and Hazelnut, Molasses Chewies, Cowboy State Peanut-Butter Chocolate-Chip, Cowpoke Cranberry-Coconut

Cowboy State Peanut-Butter Chocolate-Chip Cookies

We tend to associate peanut-butter cookies with childhood, but these are fought over by kids and adults alike, whether on the trail or at a buffet lunch, whether they're served with cold milk or fresh spring water. Unlike most peanut-butter cookies, which tend to be crumbly, these are fluffy inside, chewy around the edges, and generously speckled with nuggets of chocolate.

1 cup unsalted butter, softened
1 cup all-natural peanut butter
1 cup granulated sugar
1 cup brown sugar
2 eggs
1 teaspoon vanilla
2 cups flour
1 teaspoon salt
1 teaspoon baking soda
1 cup semisweet chocolate chips

Preheat oven to 350 degrees. Cream butter and peanut butter together; add sugars and blend well. Add eggs one at a time, then beat in vanilla. Mix flour, baking soda, and salt together, then add to batter. Mix in chocolate chips. Use ice-cream scoop to size balls of dough, placing on ungreased cookie sheets about 4" apart. Wet hands and flatten cookies with palms. Bake about 14 minutes until golden brown. Let cool on sheets until firm.

Wild Huckleberry and Hazelnut Cookies

A wild version of the traditional poppy-seed thumbprint cookies.

1 cup butter
1/2 cup sugar
2 egg yolks
1-1/2 teaspoons vanilla
2 cups flour
1/8 teaspoon salt
1 cup hazelnuts, finely chopped and
*   toasted (or walnuts, pecans,*
*   almonds)*
Huckleberry preserves (or any
*   fruit preserve)*

Cream butter and sugar in a large bowl with an electric mixer. Add yolks and vanilla and beat about 3 minutes. Add flour, salt, and nuts and blend well. Cover and chill several hours. Preheat oven to 375 degrees. Form dough into 1" balls, flatten balls slightly, and arrange 2" apart on ungreased baking sheets. Let soften for several minutes at room temperature. Make indentation in the center of each using your thumb. Bake cookies 10 to 12 minutes until lightly browned. While still warm, press centers again with your thumb. Transfer to racks. Just before serving, fill centers with fruit preserves.

Molasses Chewies

A homey old-fashioned cookie such as our pioneer forebears would have made.

3/4 cup shortening
1 cup dark brown sugar
1/4 cup blackstrap molasses
2 eggs
2 teaspoons ginger
2 teaspoons cinnamon
1 teaspoon cloves
1/2 teaspoon nutmeg
2-1/4 cups white flour
2 teaspoons baking soda
1/2 teaspoon salt

Preheat oven to 375 degrees. Cream shortening and sugar. Mix in molasses and eggs, then spices. Stir in flour, soda, and salt. Form into balls (don't be alarmed if the batter seems a little wet), then roll in sugar. Bake until tops of cookies crack, about 6 to 8 minutes.

Pine-Nut Cornmeal Biscotti

1/2 cup butter
3/4 cup sugar
3 large eggs
1 teaspoon vanilla
1 tablespoon whiskey, bourbon, or
  brandy
2 teaspoons each lemon, orange zest
1-3/4 to 2 cups flour
1 cup cornmeal
1/2 teaspoon baking powder
1/2 teaspoon baking soda
1/4 teaspoon salt
1 cup pine nuts, lightly toasted

Preheat oven to 350 degrees. Cream butter and sugar; beat in eggs one at a time. Beat in vanilla, whiskey, and zests. Sift together flour, cornmeal, baking powder, baking soda, salt, and pine nuts. Stir flour/nut mixture into batter until a dough is formed. Halve the dough.

Butter and flour a large baking sheet. With floured hands, form each half of dough into a 12" x 2" log. Place at least 3" apart on baking sheet. Press logs into baking sheet so bottom flattens slightly. Brush each log with egg wash (1 egg mixed with 1 teaspoon water). Bake for 20 to 25 minutes until golden. Cool for 10 minutes.

Transfer logs to a cutting board. Using serrated knife, cut crosswise into 1/3" slices. Arrange biscotti flat on baking sheet. Bake for 7 minutes on each side, until slightly golden. Cool biscotti on racks, then store in an airtight container.

Optional glaze: Stir together 1 cup powdered sugar, 1 tablespoon lemon juice, and 1/2 teaspoon grated lemon zest in a bowl until smooth. Spread glaze onto 1 side of each biscotti, or dip end of biscotti into glaze. Dry on racks about 20 minutes until firm.

Bittersweet Chocolate and Dried-Cherry Oat Cookies

A new twist on a legendary flavor combination, these freeze well and make a satisfying fistful on long cattle drives.

1 cup butter, softened
1 cup brown sugar
1/2 cup sugar
2 eggs
1 teaspoon vanilla
1-1/2 cups flour
1 teaspoon baking soda
1/2 teaspoon salt
3 cups rolled oats
1/2 cup dried cherries
1 cup bittersweet chocolate chips

Preheat oven to 350 degrees. Cream butter with white and brown sugars until fluffy. Mix in eggs, one at a time, and vanilla. Combine flour, baking soda, and salt on a sheet of wax paper and add to butter mixture in thirds, mixing well after each addition. Add oats, cherries, and chocolate chips until distributed evenly. Drop by rounded spoonfuls onto ungreased cookie sheet and bake 12 to 15 minutes.

Left to right: Pumpkin Harvest, Bittersweet Chocolate and Dried-Cherry Oat, Pine-Nut Cornmeal Biscotti

Pumpkin Harvest Cookies

These taste like fall and are relatively low in fat.

1/4 cup butter
1 cup brown sugar
1 egg
1 cup pumpkin puree, unsweetened
1/2 cup wheat germ, toasted
1 teaspoon baking soda
1 teaspoon baking powder
1 teaspoon cinnamon
1/2 teaspoon nutmeg
1/4 teaspoon salt
1 cup white flour
1/2 apple, unpeeled, finely chopped
1/4 cup raisins
*1/4 cup walnuts, coarsely chopped
    and toasted*

Preheat oven to 350 degrees. Grease two baking sheets. Cream butter and sugar with an electric mixer. Add egg and beat again. Then add pumpkin. Add the wheat germ, baking soda, baking powder, spices, salt, and flour and beat until mixed. Stir in apples, raisins, and walnuts.

Drop the batter by rounded teaspoonfuls about 2" apart onto prepared baking sheets. Bake 12 to 14 minutes until cookies are lightly browned. Cool on wire rack.

Chewy Coconut-Macadamia-Chocolate-Oat Cookies

As the name implies, these are wonderfully chewy from the oats, and pack the surprising crunch of exotic nuts.

2 sticks butter, softened
1 cup brown sugar
1 cup sugar
2 eggs
1 teaspoon vanilla
2 cups flour
1 teaspoon baking powder
1/2 teaspoon baking soda
1/2 teaspoon salt
1 cup rolled oats
1 cup chocolate chips
1 cup flaked coconut
1 cup macadamia nuts, chopped

Preheat oven to 375 degrees. Cream butter and sugars together, then beat in eggs and vanilla. In a separate bowl, combine dry ingredients. Add flour mixture to butter mixture, incorporating in three portions. Stir in oats, chocolate chips, coconut, and macadamia nuts. Bake large or small on ungreased cookie sheets for about 16 minutes.

Triple-Chocolate Cinnamon Cookies

1/4 cup flour
1/4 cup cocoa powder
1-1/2 teaspoons cinnamon
1/4 teaspoon baking powder
Pinch salt
6 tablespoons butter
7 tablespoons sugar
2 eggs
8 ounces semisweet chocolate, melted
    and cooled
1 cup (6 ounces) milk chocolate chips
1 cup walnuts, chopped and toasted
Garnish: walnut halves, melted semi-
    sweet chocolate (optional)

Combine flour, cocoa powder, cinnamon, baking powder, and salt in a large bowl. In s second bowl, cream butter and sugar, then beat in eggs. Stir in 8 ounces melted chocolate. Add dry mixture. Fold in milk chocolate chips and chopped walnuts. Drop dough by tablespoonfuls onto lightly greased baking sheets. Press walnut half into each. If desired, dip fork tines into melted semisweet chocolate. Wave fork over cookies, drizzling melted chocolate in zigzag pattern. Bake about 9 minutes.

Peanut- and Almond-Butter Cookies

1 cup sugar
1 cup brown sugar
1 cup butter
2 eggs, beaten
1/2 cup chunky peanut butter
1/2 cup almond butter
1 teaspoon vanilla
1 teaspoon almond extract
2-1/2 cups flour
1-1/2 teaspoons baking soda
1 teaspoon baking powder
1/2 teaspoon salt
Sugar for topping (optional)

Blend sugars, butter, eggs, peanut and almond butters, and extracts in large bowl. Sift together flour, baking soda, baking powder, and salt. Add to butter mixture and blend well. Refrigerate at least 1 hour or overnight.

Preheat oven to 375 degrees. Roll dough into walnut-size balls. Transfer to baking sheets, spacing 2" to 3" apart. Flatten each slightly with fork dipped in sugar, making a crisscross pattern. Bake until golden, 10 to 12 minutes.

Toffee Chunk Cookies

This cookie is best served with real western cowboy coffee.

1/2 cup shortening
1/2 cup butter
2 cups brown sugar
1/2 cup milk
2 eggs
3-1/2 cups white flour
1 teaspoon baking soda
1/2 teaspoon salt
1/2 cup English toffee candy bars,
   coarsely chopped
1 cup English toffee candy bars,
   in chunks

Preheat oven to 400 degrees. Cream shortening, butter, and brown sugar. Mix in milk and eggs. Stir in flour, soda, and salt until just combined. Stir in 1/2 cup chopped toffee candy. Drop dough by rounded spoonfuls onto baking sheet. Bake for 4 minutes. Pull cookie sheets out of oven and gently press two or three candy chunks into the top of each cookie. Return to oven and bake for 4 more minutes, until tops of cookies look set and have just begun to take on a golden color.

High-Desert Pecan Sandies

These simple but decadent cookies remind us of our childhood. And they're fun to make with kids, since the quantities are uniform, and rolling the dough is fun.

1 cup white sugar
1 cup powdered sugar
1 cup butter
1 cup oil
2 eggs
1 teaspoon vanilla
4-1/4 cups flour
1 teaspoon salt
1 teaspoon baking soda
1 teaspoon cream of tartar
1 cup pecans, finely chopped
   and toasted

Beat sugars, butter, oil, eggs, and vanilla thoroughly. Add flour, salt, soda, and cream of tartar. Stir in pecans. Chill dough.

Preheat oven to 375 degrees. Roll dough into balls and dip into sugar, if desired. Slightly flatten balls onto cookie sheets. Bake for 10 to 12 minutes until light brown around the edges.

Blueberry-Almond-Cornmeal Cookies

1/2 cup butter
1/2 cup sugar
1 large egg yolk
1/2 teaspoon vanilla
1/8 teaspoon almond extract
1/2 cup almonds, finely chopped
    and toasted
1/2 cup dried blueberries, finely
    chopped (may substitute apricots
    or other dried fruit)
1 cup plus 2 tablespoons white flour
1/2 cup cornmeal
1/2 teaspoon lemon zest, finely grated
Pinch salt

Cream butter and sugar. Add egg yolk and extracts; beat until fluffy. Mix in almonds and fruit. In a bowl, whisk together the flour, cornmeal, zest, and salt. Add the flour mixture to the butter mixture and stir until combined. Form the dough into a log (13" x 1-1/2") and wrap in wax paper. Chill until firm, about 3 hours.

Preheat oven to 400 degrees. Lightly grease baking sheets. Cut the dough into 1/4" thick rounds and arrange 1" apart on prepared baking sheets. Bake until edges become golden, about 10 minutes. Cool on racks.

Stacked: Blueberry-Almond-Cornmeal; plate: High-Desert Pecan Sandies, Glazed Apple Gems

Glazed Apple Gems

Cookies:

1/2 cup butter
1-1/3 cups brown sugar
1 egg
1 teaspoon vanilla
1 large apple, finely chopped
1 cup golden raisins, finely chopped
1 teaspoon lemon peel, finely grated
2 cups flour
1 teaspoon baking soda
1 teaspoon cinnamon
1/2 teaspoon nutmeg
1 cup walnuts, toasted and finely
 chopped

Glaze:

1 cup powdered sugar
2 tablespoons apple juice
1 tablespoon lemon juice
1 tablespoon butter, melted and
 cooled

Preheat oven to 375 degrees. Cream butter and sugar in large bowl until light and fluffy. Beat in egg. Stir in apple, raisins, and lemon peel. Blend in flour, baking soda, cinnamon, and nutmeg, then walnuts until just combined. Drop dough by tablespoonfuls onto lightly greased baking sheets. Bake 12 minutes. Cool on rack 10 minutes.

Meanwhile, prepare glaze. Blend sugar, juices, and butter in a blender or processor. Spoon glaze onto cookies, allowing extra to drip off. Finish cooling on rack.

Oversized Apricot-Pecan-Oatmeal Cookies

This is a great cookie to munch on a hike or trail ride.

3 sticks butter, softened
1 cup dark brown sugar, firmly packed
3/4 cup sugar
2 large eggs, room temperature
1 teaspoon vanilla
2 cups unbleached all-purpose flour
1-1/2 teaspoons baking soda
1-1/2 teaspoons cinnamon
1/2 teaspoon nutmeg
1/4 teaspoon allspice
4 cups rolled oats
1 cup chopped apricots
1 cup chopped pecans

Preheat oven to 375 degrees. Cream butter and sugars together until light in color and texture. Beat in eggs, one by one, until well incorporated, then add vanilla. Combine the flour, baking soda, and spices together and sift into the wet ingredients. Stir in the oats, apricots, and pecans. Moisten hands and roll balls a little larger than a golf ball. Place on ungreased cookie sheets 4" apart. Bake for 12 to 14 minutes. Cool for 2 minutes on cookie sheet, then remove to wire rack.

Breteche Bars

If the Toll House cookie is the first thing an American child learns to bake, the brownie is undoubtedly the second. Like the chocolate-chip cookie, the brownie, the original bar cookie, is distinctly American. As such, there are few things that last better in a saddlebag or in a picnic basket, on a sailing trip, at the soccer match, or in your child's lunch box. And there are few things that taste better.

Brownies have grown up. One used to choose between brownies or brownies with nuts. If someone really didn't like chocolate (and that of course could only be if one were allergic to it, because who would willingly refuse chocolate?), there were always blondies, but people were not generally proud of blondies.

Times have changed. Here we offer brownies, blondies we can be proud of, and a multitude of interesting alternatives, including the ultimate and ultimately simple butterscotch brownie, a fudge brownie with a pecan-graham crust that's worthy of a White House tea, apricot bars made with dried fruit rather than preserves, and many other options for those tired of the same old thing. As with our cookies, don't be afraid to use these recipes as a starting point for your own creative combinations!

Breteche Blondies

Pecans, coconut, and chocolate chips give the age-old blondie an interesting taste and texture.

1 cup flour
3/4 teaspoon baking soda
1/4 teaspoon salt
1 egg
1 cup brown sugar
1-1/2 teaspoons vanilla
1/2 cup butter, melted
1 cup milk chocolate chips
1 cup grated coconut
1 cup pecans, toasted and chopped

Preheat oven to 350 degrees. Butter an 8 x 8" baking pan. Sift dry ingredients together and set aside. Beat egg with brown sugar for several minutes until batter appears light-colored and slightly frothy. Add vanilla and melted butter until just incorporated, then mix in dry ingredients, chips, coconut, and nuts. Bake 20 to 30 minutes until top seems dry and blondies take on a light brown color.

Fresh Apple Bars

A wholesome bar whose layered apple slices make for an artistic presentation.

1 cup white flour
1/2 cup whole-wheat flour
1 cup rolled oats
1 cup dark brown sugar
2 teaspoons lemon zest, grated
3/4 teaspoon baking powder
1/2 teaspoon salt
1/2 cup soft butter
1/4 cup orange juice concentrate, thawed
2 medium tart apples, peeled, cored, and thinly sliced
1/4 cup walnuts, coarsely chopped and toasted

Preheat oven to 350 degrees. Lightly butter an 8 x 8" baking pan. In a large bowl, combine flours, oats, sugar, lemon zest, baking powder, and salt. Work in butter and orange- juice concentrate with your fingers until dough forms. Firmly press half of the oat mixture into prepared pan. Arrange apples slices evenly over crust. Mix walnuts into remaining oat mixture. Sprinkle mixture over apples and press into an even layer. Bake until top is lightly browned, about 30 to 35 minutes. Cool completely in pan on wire rack. Cut into squares.

Left: Fresh Apple Bars, Backpacker Bars, Pure Butterscotch Brownies

Pure Butterscotch Brownies

These have a wonderful butterscotch flavor and a chewy texture. Kids love 'em.

1 cup (6 ounces) butterscotch chips
1/4 cup butter
1 cup brown sugar
2 beaten eggs
1/2 teaspoon vanilla
1 cup flour
1 teaspoon baking powder
3/4 teaspoon salt

Preheat oven to 350 degrees. Melt chips and butter together over hot (not boiling) water. Remove from heat and stir in the brown sugar. Let cool for five minutes, then blend in the eggs and vanilla.

Sift together dry ingredients and combine the two mixtures. Spread in a greased and floured 8 x 8" pan. Bake for 30 to 35 minutes until golden brown.

Backpacker Bars

A heavy, intense, and delicious bar that holds up well in your pack—and in your stomach.

1 cup butter
1-1/2 cups brown sugar
1 cup rolled oats
1 cup whole-wheat flour
1 cup all-purpose flour
1/2 cup wheat germ
4 teaspoons orange peel, freshly grated
4 eggs
2 cups whole almonds
1 cup semisweet chocolate chips
1/2 cup dates, chopped
1/2 cup dried apricots, chopped
1/2 cup coconut, shredded or flaked

Preheat oven to 350 degrees. Cream butter with 1 cup brown sugar in large bowl. Stir in oats, flours, wheat germ, and orange peel. Spread mixture evenly in bottom of 9 x 13" baking pan. Combine eggs, almonds, chocolate chips, dates, apricots, coconut, and remaining 1/2 cup brown sugar in another large bowl and mix gently. Pour over butter mixture, spreading evenly. Bake until browned, about 30 to 35 minutes. Let cool. Cut into bars.

Almond Cream-Cheese Brownies

Brownies:

3 ounces unsweetened chocolate
6 tablespoons butter
1-1/2 cups sugar
3 eggs
1/4 teaspoon salt
3/4 cup flour
3/4 teaspoon almond extract

Cream-Cheese Layer:

8 ounces cream cheese
1/3 cup sugar
1 egg
1/2 teaspoon almond extract
1/3 cup slivered almonds

Preheat oven to 350 degrees. Butter an 8 x 8" baking dish. For chocolate base, melt chocolate and butter together in double boiler or microwave and stir. Remove from heat. In large bowl, stir together sugar, eggs, salt, flour, and almond extract. Add chocolate-butter mixture and mix well. Spread in buttered pan.

In medium bowl, beat cream cheese until smooth, then beat in sugar, egg, and almond extract. Pour over chocolate layer in pan, then draw lines through top with a knife, first in one direction, then in other, to create a marbled design. Scatter almonds over top. Bake 40 to 45 minutes until cheese layer is lightly browned and brownies seem firm to touch.

Layered Pumpkin Pie Squares

Crust:

3/4 cup white flour
1/2 cup whole-wheat flour
1/2 cup dark brown sugar
1/2 tablespoon baking powder
1/2 teaspoon salt
5 tablespoons unsalted butter, chilled
1 egg yolk
2 teaspoons milk

Topping:

2 tablespoons dark brown sugar
1/2 teaspoon cinnamon
1 tablespoon butter, chilled
1/2 cup walnuts, chopped and toasted

Filling:

1 large egg
2 tablespoons sugar
2 tablespoons dark brown sugar
1-3/4 cups pumpkin puree
2 teaspoons molasses
1/3 cup half-and-half
1 teaspoon cinnamon
1/2 teaspoon ginger
1/4 teaspoon allspice
1/8 teaspoon each nutmeg, cloves, salt

Preheat oven to 350 degrees. Lightly grease an 8 x 8" baking pan.

Prepare crust by sifting flours, sugar, baking powder, and salt into a large bowl. Cut butter into pieces and mix into flour mixture until it resembles coarse crumbs. Reserve 1/2 cup of mixture for topping. Beat egg yolk and milk together, add to remaining crumb mixture, then press crumb mixture evenly into bottom of pan. Bake 15 minutes. Cool.

Add sugar and cinnamon to saved crumb mixture. Cut in butter until crumbly. Mix in walnuts; set aside.

For filling, whisk egg in large bowl until frothy. Add sugars and stir until dissolved. Gradually add pumpkin, molasses, and half-and-half; mix until smooth. Stir in spices and salt. Pour filling into prepared crust. Cover with topping. Bake until filling is set in center and topping is golden brown, about 30 minutes. Cool on rack. Top with whipped cream or ice cream.

S'more Bars

S'mores without the campfire!

Crust:
1-1/4 cups graham-cracker crumbs
1/4 cup flour
1/4 cup brown sugar
1/4 cup butter, melted

Topping:
1/3 cup heavy whipping cream
1 cup (6 ounces) milk chocolate chips
1-1/2 cups miniature marshmallows

Preheat oven to 350 degrees. For crust, combine crumbs, flour, and brown sugar in a medium bowl. Stir in melted butter. Pour crumb mixture into an ungreased 8 x 8" pan and press firmly to evenly cover the bottom of the pan. Bake for 15 minutes. Cool before topping.

For topping, heat cream in heavy medium saucepan until just simmering; remove from heat. Add chocolate; whisk slowly until melted, scraping bottom of pan with rubber spatula occasionally. As soon as mixture becomes smooth, pour over prepared crust. Scatter marshmallows evenly across chocolate and place pan under broiler for a few seconds to begin to melt the marshmallows, being careful not to burn the chocolate. Cool before cutting.

Fudge Bars with Pecan-Graham Crust

Crust:

(5) 5 x 2-1/2" graham crackers,
   or 2/3 cup graham-cracker crumbs
1/2 cup pecans, toasted
2 tablespoons sugar
6 tablespoons butter, melted
1/2 teaspoon salt

Fudge Layer:

4 ounces unsweetened chocolate,
   chopped
1/2 cup butter
2 eggs, beaten
1/4 teaspoon vanilla
1/4 teaspoon salt
2 cups brown sugar
1 cup flour

Preheat oven to 350 degrees. Make crust by crumbling graham crackers into food processor and grinding into crumbs. Add pecans, sugar, butter, and salt and pulse motor until nuts are chopped fine. Press crumb mixture evenly onto bottom of an 7 x 11" baking pan and bake in middle of oven for 5 minutes. Cool crust in pan on a rack.

Make fudge in a double boiler (or medium metal bowl set over a saucepan of barely simmering water) by melting chocolate with butter and stirring. Remove bowl from pan and cool to room temperature. Beat in remaining ingredients until smooth.

Spread fudge layer on top of crust and bake for 30 to 35 minutes or until top is set and edges have begun to pull away from sides of pan. While fudge is still hot, cut into 24 small bars with a sharp knife. Cool bars in pan on rack.

Chocolate Shortbread Turtles

Shortbread:

1 cup flour
1/2 cup brown sugar
1 tablespoon unsweetened cocoa
  powder
1/2 teaspoon baking soda
Pinch of salt
1/2 cup butter, melted

Caramel-Pecan Topping:

3/4 cup white sugar
1/3 cup light corn syrup
3 tablespoons water
Pinch salt
1/3 cup heavy cream
1 teaspoon vanilla
1-1/2 cups whole pecans

Preheat oven to 350 degrees. Prepare shortbread by combining flour, sugar, cocoa powder, soda, and salt in a large bowl. Stir in butter. Press mixture into ungreased 8 x 8" baking pan. Bake in preheated oven until set, about 15 minutes.

Prepare caramel in a heavy 3-quart saucepan by bringing sugar, corn syrup, water, and salt to a boil over moderate heat, stirring until sugar is dissolved. Boil mixture, without stirring, until it begins to turn a golden caramel color, about 10 to 15 minutes. Remove pan from heat; let cool a minute. While briskly stirring, slowly pour in cream and vanilla. Mixture will bubble and steam. If clumps form, place pan on low heat and stir until they melt. Do not boil! Stir in pecans. Quickly pour over shortbread. Cool at least 4 hours until caramel is firm.

Left: Chocolate Shortbread Turtles, Fudge Bars with Pecan-Graham Crust

Dried-Apricot Bars

Apricot Filling:

1 cup water
1-1/2 cups dried apricots, chopped
    (or substitute dried nectarines,
    peaches, or plums)
1/4 cup sugar

Base:

1 cup butter
1 cup brown sugar
1-1/2 cups flour
1 cup rolled oats, ground in a
    food processor
1/2 cup wheat germ

Preheat oven to 350 degrees. Lightly butter an 8 x 8" baking dish. Combine water, chopped apricots, and sugar in a small saucepan and bring to a boil. Cook over medium heat for 15 to 20 minutes until liquid has been absorbed. Set aside to cool.

Make base by creaming butter with brown sugar, then mixing in flour, oats, and wheat germ. Press half of mixture into prepared dish to make an even layer. Bake for 20 minutes until golden brown. Set aside to cool.

Carefully distribute apricots across the top of the baked base. Layer topping over apricots and press down gently. Bake for approximately 30 minutes until light brown on top. Let cool before slicing. Makes 16 bars.

Peanut Butter and Jelly Bars

Fun for kids to make and to eat!

1/2 cup butter
3/4 cup crunchy peanut butter
1/2 cup sugar
1/2 cup light brown sugar
1 egg
1 teaspoon vanilla
1-1/4 cups white flour
3/4 teaspoon baking soda
1/2 teaspoon baking powder
3/4 cup jelly or jam, any kind

Preheat oven to 350 degrees. Cream butter, peanut butter, and sugars. Beat in egg and vanilla. Stir in flour, baking soda, and baking powder. Reserve 1 cup dough. Press remaining dough in an ungreased 13 x 9" pan. Spread with jelly. Crumble reserved dough over jelly. Bake until golden brown, about 25 minutes. Cool completely.

Comforting Custards, Cobblers and Crisps

Starting in June with long stalks of tart rhubarb and continuing on through Labor Day with peaches, plums, watermelon, cherries, and a host of berries, fruit defines the summer season. When twilight falls by dinnertime and the fleece jackets stay on 'til mid-morning, we know autumn is on its way, and with it, steaming desserts of apples, cranberries, and the like to take us right through winter.

For its fullest, sweetest impact, fruit is best eaten unadorned. But fruit is also wonderful when cooked. Cobblers and crisps are what we like best. They are universally appealing, casual but always impressive, and able to stand up to a ranch-sized crowd. With a quick toss of flour and sugar, a dotting of butter, and a biscuit or batter topping, baked fruit takes on a heady aroma, a deep flavor, and a soul-soothing essence that satisfies through the ages.

For pure comfort food, we think it's a toss-up between cobblers and crisps and that family of decadent desserts, custards. The purest versions have a long history and are found, with regional variations, in many cuisines. These traditional preparations forego complex flavors for the mellow smoothness of a creamy egg-and-milk concoction. They go down so easily, in fact, that they were historically offered up to invalids. In recent years, custards have reappeared on menus nationwide, prompting their renewed popularity in home kitchens, and no wonder: Custards fill the tummy, warm the spirit, and are simple to prepare. Better yet, contemporary versions don't necessarily depend on heavy cream for their character, but can be made with regular milk and even egg whites. Cobblers, crisps, and custards from your kitchen—they give new meaning to the phrase "all the comforts of home."

Apple-Cranberry Country Cobbler

Autumn in the northern Rockies comes unmistakably in mid-August: in the angle of the sun, the way the skies darken ever earlier, and a decided chill to the evenings. We find August none too early for this apple-and-cranberry combination.

Fruit:

3 to 4 tart apples, peeled, cored, and sliced
1/2 package cranberries
1/2 cup sugar
1/4 cup all-purpose flour
1/2 teaspoon cinnamon
1/4 teaspoon allspice
1/8 teaspoon nutmeg

Topping:

1-1/4 cups all-purpose flour
1/4 cup whole-wheat flour
1/2 cup sugar
1/2 teaspoon salt
1 teaspoon baking powder
1/4 teaspoon cinnamon
1/4 cup unsalted butter, melted and cooled
1/2 cup milk
1 tablespoon sugar
1/8 teaspoon nutmeg

Preheat oven to 350 degrees. Mix the fruit, sugar, flour, and spices together and pour into a 9 x 13" glass or ceramic baking dish. In a bowl, sift the flours, sugar, salt, baking powder, cinnamon. Mix the milk and butter together and fold into dry ingredients until smooth. Spoon the batter over the fruit, spreading to the edges of the dish. Combine the remaining tablespoon of sugar with the nutmeg and sprinkle across the top. Bake the cobbler for 45 to 60 minutes. Let cool for at least 10 minutes, then serve with vanilla ice cream or whipped cream.

Strawberry-Rhubarb Cobbler
with Cornmeal-Buttermilk-Biscuit Topping

Fruit:

4 cups fresh strawberries, sliced
  (or frozen unsweetened, thawed,
  and drained)
4 cups fresh rhubarb, sliced
  (or frozen unsweetened, thawed,
  and drained)
1/2 cup sugar, depending on tartness
2 tablespoons flour
1 teaspoon lemon juice

Topping:

3/4 cup flour
1/2 cup cornmeal
2 tablespoons sugar
1 teaspoon baking powder
1/2 teaspoon baking soda
1/2 teaspoon salt
4 tablespoons butter, chilled
1/2 cup buttermilk

Sugar-cinnamon mixture for
  topping (optional)

Preheat the oven to 425 degrees. Butter an 8 x 8" baking dish. Toss the strawberries, rhubarb, sugar, flour, and lemon juice together. Pour into prepared baking dish. Sift together flour, cornmeal, sugar, baking powder, baking soda, and salt. Cut the butter into the flour mixture with pastry knife or fingers until mixture resembles coarse crumbs. Stir in buttermilk until dough forms. Turn the dough onto a floured surface and roll it out to a square large enough to cover the fruit. (Dough may seem a little wet.) Place the dough on top of the fruit, then sprinkle with a mixture of sugar and cinnamon, if desired. Bake for 30 minutes, or until slightly browned. Serve warm with ice cream or heavy cream.

Right: Strawberry-Rhubarb Cobbler
with Cornmeal-Buttermilk-Biscuit Topping

Lemon-Pear Crunch

A delightful variation on baked apple desserts, this one sings with the fresh taste of lemon.

Filling:

4 pounds (about 6 medium) pears,
  coarsely chopped
1/2 cup lemon juice
3/4 cup brown sugar
1 tablespoon flour

Topping:

1 cup rolled oats
1 cup flour
2/3 cup brown sugar
Zest of 1 lemon
1/2 teaspoon cinnamon
1/4 teaspoon salt
3/4 cup unsalted butter, chilled and
  cut into 1/4" pieces

Preheat oven to 400 degrees. Toss chopped pears, lemon juice, sugar, and flour together. Place in a large baking pan (9 x 13") or a large pie plate (12" round). Mix oats, flour, brown sugar, lemon zest, cinnamon, and salt. Add the butter and cut into flour mixture with a pastry cutter or rub in with your fingers until the mixture resembles coarse crumbs. Sprinkle the topping over the pears. Bake for 30 to 35 minutes. Let cool on rack for at least 10 minutes before serving.

Pannetone Bread Pudding
with Apricot–Triple Sec Sauce

Bread Pudding:

5 cups pannetone, cut in 3/4" cubes
* and lightly toasted (or use challah*
* or croissants)*
2 cups whipping cream
1/2 cup half-and-half
5 egg yolks
1/2 cup plus 2 tablespoons sugar
1/4 teaspoon vanilla

Preheat oven to 325 degrees. Place 6 ramekins in a large baking dish. Divide toasted bread cubes between them. Heat cream and half-and-half in a heavy saucepan over moderate flame, bringing just to a simmer.

Whisk egg yolks and sugar together in a bowl. Slowly whisk the hot cream into the mixture. Stir in vanilla and divide mixture among ramekins. Create a water bath by filling baking dish until water comes halfway up the sides of the ramekins. Bake for 40 minutes until custard appears set. Let cool slightly. Serve with a little sauce poured over each bread pudding; pass remainder in small pitcher.

Apricot–Triple Sec Sauce:

2 cups dried apricots, finely chopped
1/2 cup water
1/4 cup Triple Sec
1/4 cup sugar
1/2 teaspoon vanilla

In a medium saucepan, combine apricots, water, Triple Sec, and sugar. Cover and cook over medium heat until apricots are tender, 10 to 15 minutes. Stir in vanilla and more Triple Sec, if desired. Recipe can be made ahead and served warm or cold.

Lemon Crème Brûlée

A lower fat version of the French classic, updated with the fresh zing of lemon. This can be made in individual ramekins or in one baking dish.

1 cup cream
1 cup milk
4 egg yolks
2 eggs
1/2 cup sugar
6 ounces raspberries (optional)
1/2 teaspoon lemon juice
1/2 teaspoon lemon zest,
*   finely chopped*
4 tablespoons brown sugar

Preheat oven to 300 degrees. Scald cream and milk in saucepan until hot and simmering around edges. (Don't let it boil.) Beat egg yolks and whole eggs with sugar in bowl. Slowly add warm cream and milk mixture to sugar and egg mixture, whisking continuously. Whisk in lemon juice.

Set four ramekins in baking dish large enough to hold them comfortably. If using raspberries, distribute them evenly among the ramekins. Pour custard into ramekins, dividing evenly. Sprinkle lemon zest on top. Bake for about an hour, until custard is set. Let cool on counter, then refrigerate.

Before serving, carefully spread one tablespoon brown sugar across the top of each ramekin to make an even layer. Put under the broiler and watch closely, removing when sugar has melted.

Right: Lemon Crème Brûlée

Maple Crème Caramel

1-1/3 cups pure maple syrup
2 cups milk
(do not use lowfat or nonfat milk)
3 large eggs
2 egg yolks

Preheat oven to 350 degrees. Cook 1 cup syrup in heavy 2-quart saucepan over medium-low heat until reduced to 3/4 cup, stirring constantly, about 10 minutes. Immediately pour syrup into six 3/4-cup ramekins.

Scald milk in large, heavy saucepan. Whisk eggs, yolks, and remaining 1/3 cup syrup in medium bowl to blend. Gradually whisk in hot milk. Strain custard. Ladle into syrup-lined ramekins.

Place ramekins in large baking pan. Add enough boiling water to pan to come halfway up sides of ramekins. Bake until custards move slightly in center when pan is shaken, about 35 minutes. Remove custards from water. Cover and refrigerate until well chilled. Run small sharp knife around custards to loosen. Unmold onto plates (some of syrup may have crystallized) and serve.

Pumpkin Bread Pudding with Pecan-Caramel Sauce

Pumpkin Bread:

1-1/4 cups sugar

1/2 cup vegetable oil

2 large eggs

1 cup solid pack pumpkin

1-1/2 cups all-purpose flour

1/4 teaspoon baking powder

1/2 teaspoon baking soda

1/4 teaspoon salt

2 teaspoons cinnamon

1/4 teaspoon cloves

1/2 teaspoon nutmeg

Raisins (optional)

Preheat oven to 350 degrees. Butter and flour a 9 x 5" loaf pan. Combine sugar and oil in large bowl. Beat in eggs one at a time, then mix in pumpkin. Sift together flour, baking powder, baking soda, salt, and spices. Stir into pumpkin mixture in two additions. Stir in optional raisins.

Bake until tester inserted in center comes out clean, about 1 hour. Cool bread in pan 10 minutes. Turn out onto rack and cool completely.

Bread Pudding:

5 large eggs

1/2 cup sugar

2 cups half-and-half

1-1/2 cups canned evaporated milk

1 tablespoon vanilla

1 loaf pumpkin bread, cut into
   1" cubes

Preheat oven to 350 degrees. Grease 13 x 9" baking pan. Beat eggs in medium bowl until frothy. Mix in sugar. Gradually mix in half-and-half, evaporated milk, and vanilla. Put

(cont'd)

bread cubes into prepared pan. Pour milk mixture over and mix gently. Bake pudding about 1 hour until tester inserted near center comes out clean; cover pudding loosely with foil if browning too quickly. Cool slightly.

Pecan-Caramel Sauce:

Makes about 1-1/2 cups and can be prepared ahead; cover and refrigerate, then rewarm slowly over low heat before serving.

1/2 cup butter, cut into pieces
1/2 cup brown sugar
1/2 cup sugar
1/2 cup whole milk
   (do not use lowfat or skim milk)
1 teaspoon vanilla
1/2 cup pecans, chopped and toasted

Combine butter, brown sugar, sugar, and milk in heavy medium saucepan. Stir over low heat until sugar dissolves and butter melts. Increase heat and boil 1 minute. Remove from heat. Mix in vanilla and nuts.

Pour a thin layer of Pecan Caramel Sauce over bread pudding. Pass the extra sauce with individual servings.

Right: Pumpkin Bread Pudding with Pecan-Caramel Sauce

Surprise Endings

What is a surprise ending? Basically anything that's unexpected. The good guy doesn't always get the girl and go riding off into the sunset. And sometimes it's more memorable that way.

A surprise ending to a meal can be an assortment of cheeses, a retro dessert like bananas flambé, or a bowl of perfectly ripe raspberries with no adornment but a sprig of mint. In the recipes that follow, it can be a soufflé made with Grand Marnier, a steamed pudding laced with spiced pecans and whiskey, a chocolate cake layered with banana mousse, or an endearing little bundle made to look like a hobo's kit tied up in a bandana.

In this section, ten restaurants around the Rockies offer their innovative versions of new western desserts. For the most dramatic of grand finales, try the Caramel Apple Tartlets covered by a latticework of hardened caramel (see pp. 66–67). This, after all, is where we stretch our wings.

Don't be afraid to surprise yourself. Experimenting is great fun, even if it does result in a disaster or two. It's the unexpected that keeps life interesting.

Cafe Carrot Cake

The Park Cafe, St. Mary, Montana

St. Mary, Montana, next to Glacier National Park, is home to this recipe as well as pies famous throughout the region.

Cake:

1-3/4 cups brown sugar
2 cups white flour
1 cup whole-wheat flour
1 teaspoon baking soda
2 teaspoons baking powder
1 teaspoon salt
2 teaspoons cinnamon
1 teaspoon nutmeg
1 teaspoon allspice
1 cup oil
4 eggs, beaten
2 teaspoons vanilla
3 cups grated carrots, soaked in
   3 tablespoons lemon juice

Cream-Cheese Frosting:

8 ounces cream cheese, softened
1/2 cup butter
1 box powdered sugar (about 2 cups)
2 teaspoons vanilla
1 cup walnuts, chopped

To make cake, mix brown sugar, flours, baking powder, baking soda, salt, and spices, being sure to break up any brown sugar lumps. Add oil and mix well. Add beaten eggs, vanilla, and then carrots soaked in lemon juice. Pour batter into a greased 9 x 13" baking dish. Bake 30 minutes or until the cake feels firm to the touch and has taken on a golden-brown color. Let cool.

To make frosting, beat cream cheese and butter together. Gradually add powdered sugar, then the vanilla and walnuts. (Use half the amount of frosting for a less rich cake.)

Frozen Tequila-Lime Pie

The Gallatin Gateway Inn, Gallatin Gateway, Montana

The Gallatin Gateway Inn has been serving western cuisine since 1927, when it opened as the first railroad hotel outside a national park. Recently restored, the inn features superb views in a setting of western-style casual elegance.

Crust:

1-1/4 cups graham-cracker crumbs
1/4 cup sugar
1/3 cup butter, melted

Preheat oven to 375 degrees. Mix graham-cracker crumbs, 1/4 cup sugar, and melted butter together in bowl. Using back of a large spoon, press mixture firmly into bottom and sides of an 8" or 9" pie plate. Bake for 6 to 8 minutes until light brown. Set aside to cool.

Filling:

3 eggs, separated
1/2 cup sugar
Zest and juice of 1 large lime
1 cup heavy cream
2 to 4 tablespoons Jose Cuervo or other good-quality tequila

Using an electric mixer, beat egg yolks with 1/2 cup sugar until yolks are pale. Blend in lime juice and zest. In separate mixing bowl, beat egg whites until stiff but not dry. Fold whites into yolk mixture. Add tequila to taste. Pour mixture into prepared graham cracker crust and freeze overnight.

Serve with slices of lime, fresh strawberries, and a sprig of mint.

Individual Grand Marnier Soufflés

The Sun Valley Lodge, Sun Valley, Idaho

Chef Scott Walmsley's soufflé symbolizes the Sun Valley experience: a true classic flavored with a taste of Europe and presented with a flourish.

2 ounces butter, softened
2 ounces sugar
22 ounces whole milk (almost 3 cups)
1/2 pound butter, chopped into
*   small pieces*
Pinch salt
Grated zest of 1 orange
10 ounces flour (about 2-1/2 cups)
5 ounces sugar (a little over 1/2 cup)
10 eggs, separated
1 teaspoon vanilla
2 ounces Grand Marnier
Powdered sugar

Place rack below center of oven and preheat to 375 degrees. Coat insides of 10 ramekins with softened butter. Add sugar to the dish and roll around to coat. Tap out excess.

In a saucepan, bring milk, salt, butter, and zest to a simmer. Mix the flour and sugar together and add all at once. Stir rapidly until mixture forms a ball and comes away from the sides of the pan. Remove from heat.

Separate eggs; place yolks in large bowl and whites in a mixing bowl. One spoonful at a time, add soufflé mixture to egg yolks, stirring, then mix in Grand Marnier and vanilla.

Whip the egg whites to soft peaks. Fold them into the base, one-third at a time. Divide the mixture evenly among ramekins and gently tap on the counter to remove air pockets.

Bake for 30 to 35 minutes until the soufflés are almost twice the size of the cups and have taken on a golden-brown color. Remove from the oven and dust with powdered sugar. Serve with a sauce anglaise, if desired.

Steamed Whiskey Pudding

Maxwell's Restaurant, Cody, Wyoming

Maxwell's offers an interesting variety of fresh dishes, great scones, delicious breads—and killer desserts.

Filling:

1/4 pound unsalted butter
2 cups sugar
6 eggs
1 tablespoon vanilla
2 cups all-purpose flour
1/2 teaspoon salt
1 teaspoon soda
2 teaspoons baking powder
2 cups Spicy Pecans, chopped
1/2 cup bourbon

Preheat oven to 350 degrees. Lightly grease the inside of a 9 x 13" cake pan and dust with flour. Cream butter and sugar. Add eggs one at a time, then vanilla. Sift dry ingredients, then add to egg/butter mixture. Add pecans and bourbon and mix well.

Pour batter into prepared pan. Place cake pan in larger pan. Add enough water to come halfway up the sides of the cake pan. Cover with foil. Bake about 40 minutes until set in the center. Pudding will fall some after being removed from the oven. Serve warm with whipped cream, ice cream, zabaglione, or whiskeyed creme anglaise.

Spicy Pecans:

2 cups pecans, lightly toasted
1/2 cup brown sugar
2 tablespoons cinnamon
1 teaspoon nutmeg
1/8 teaspoon cloves
2 tablespoons butter
2 tablespoons vanilla

Mix sugar and spices together and sprinkle evenly over nuts. Dot with butter. Bake 7 to 8 minutes at 350 degrees, stirring once. Sprinkle vanilla over hot pecans, stirring to coat. Bake 5 to 8 minutes more. Let cool.

Right: Steamed Whiskey Pudding

Strawberries
with Molasses Sour-Cream Sauce

Fresh fruit makes for simple, summery desserts. The addition of this molasses-tinged sauce adds visual interest as well as the taste of pioneer days.

1/2 cup sour cream
1/2 teaspoon sugar
1/8 teaspoon vanilla
2 tablespoons molasses
1 pint strawberries, halved

In a small bowl, whisk together sour cream, sugar, vanilla, and 1 tablespoon molasses until smooth. Divide strawberries between 2 bowls and top with sour-cream sauce. Drizzle remaining molasses over servings.

Minted Berry Spongecakes

Fruit:

1/2 cup water
2/3 cup sugar
1/2 cup fresh mint leaves, packed
1-1/2 tablespoons fresh lemon juice
1-1/2 pints fresh berries

In a small saucepan bring water and sugar to a boil, stirring until sugar is dissolved. Add mint and simmer 1 minute. Remove pan from heat and crush mint against pan with a wooden spoon. Let syrup stand, covered, 20 minutes. Pour through a fine sieve into a bowl, pressing on mint. Add lemon juice and berries. Let mixture stand for 30 minutes to blend flavors.

Individual Spongecakes for 9:

2 large eggs
1/3 cup sugar
1/3 cup all-purpose flour
1 tablespoon cornstarch
3 tablespoons unsalted butter,
  melted and cooled slightly

Preheat oven to 350 degrees; line nine 1/2-cup muffin tins with paper liners. In a metal bowl set over a saucepan of barely simmering water, whisk together eggs and sugar until sugar is dissolved, 1 to 2 minutes. Remove bowl from heat; beat mixture at moderate speed until doubled in volume, about 3 minutes. Sift flour, cornstarch, and a pinch of salt over egg mixture; fold in gently. Drizzle butter over batter; fold in gently. Divide batter among tins and bake in middle of oven 12 to 15 minutes until pale golden. Cool spongecakes in tins for 10 minutes. Remove and cool completely on rack.

To serve: Halve spongecakes horizontally. Put spongecake bottoms on six plates, spoon berry mixture over them, then sour cream. Arrange spongecake tops on desserts.

Applesauce Gingerbread
with Caramelized Apples and Whipped Cream

Gingerbread:

3 cups flour
2 teaspoons baking soda
1 teaspoon cinnamon
1/4 teaspoon ground cloves
1/4 teaspoon ginger
1/2 teaspoon salt
1 cup butter, melted
1 cup brown sugar
1/2 cup molasses
1 cup applesauce
2 eggs
1 teaspoon fresh ginger, grated
1/2 cup boiling water

Preheat oven to 350 degrees. Sift together all dry ingredients. Combine butter, sugar, molasses, applesauce, eggs, and ginger, then stir together with dry ingredients. Add water and mix until very smooth. Pour into a greased and floured bundt pan. Bake approximately 50 minutes, testing for doneness with a toothpick.

Caramelized Apples for 4:

3 medium apples (or two large),
    peeled, cored, and thinly sliced
2 tablespoons butter
3 tablespoons brown sugar

Melt butter, then add apples slices and sauté until they begin to soften. When pan is hot, add brown sugar, cooking over high heat until the sugar starts to caramelize and the apples are browned with a slightly burnt look on the edges.

Serve each thick wedge of cake with a pile of apples nestled up against it and a large dollop of whipped cream on top.

*Right: Applesauce Gingerbread
with Caramelized Apples and Whipped Cream*

Chocolate Banana-Mousse Cake

Spanish Peaks Brewery, Bozeman, Montana

Chocolate Cake:

3 cups plus 2 tablespoons flour
3 cups sugar
1/3 cup plus 2 teaspoons cocoa powder
1-1/2 teaspoons baking soda
1/3 teaspoon salt
6 ounces unsalted butter, melted
1-1/2 cups cold water
3/4 cup vegetable oil
3 large eggs
3/4 cup buttermilk
1-1/2 teaspoons vanilla

To prepare cake, preheat oven to 350 degrees. Butter and flour two 9"-round cake pans. Sift dry ingredients into a large mixing bowl. Combine liquid ingredients and add to dry mixture until just combined. Batter will be quite thin. Pour into prepared cake pans. Bake about 20 minutes until edges of cake pull away from sides and the center springs back lightly.

Banana Mousse:

2 ounces unsalted butter
1/2 cup sugar
3 bananas, cut into 1-1/2" pieces
Juice of 1/4 of a lemon
1 cup heavy whipping cream
1 teaspoon vanilla
2 teaspoons powdered gelatin
3 tablespoons cold water, rum,
  or orange juice
3 eggs, separated

Melt butter in a sauté pan over medium-high heat. Add sugar and stir until sugar dissolves. Add bananas and lemon juice; cook until bananas are just soft, about 3 to 6 minutes. Puree, pour into large bowl; set aside.

In a medium saucepan, soften gelatin in the liquid for 5 minutes, stirring to remove lumps. Whip the cream and vanilla until it holds peaks. Chill. Dissolve the softened gelatin over low heat. Stir 1/3 of the bananas into warm gelatin, then combine with the rest of the bananas. Chill over larger bowl filled with ice water until cool and thick, stirring to prevent lumping.

Place a small saucepan 1/4 full of water on burner and bring to simmer. Place egg yolks in a bowl and hold over saucepan, whisking continuously. Do not let the egg bowl touch water. Continue whisking until the yolks get thick and pale in color.

Whisk 1/4 of the chilled banana mixture into the egg yolks until smooth, then whisk in another 1/4 until smooth, then add remaining bananas and whisk until smooth. Whip egg whites until they hold a peak. Fold into banana mixture in three additions. Fold whipped cream into banana mixture in 3 additions. Cover tightly and chill until set, about 4 hours. (This can be prepared a day ahead.)

Chocolate Glaze:

1-1/2 cups heavy whipping cream
12 ounces good-quality bittersweet chocolate, chopped into pieces

Place chocolate in a bowl. Bring cream to a boil in a small saucepan; pour over chocolate and let sit for a few minutes. Stir until smooth.

Remove cooled cakes from pans. With a serrated knife, cut each cake in half. Using only 3 of the 4 layers, spread 1/4 of the banana mousse over the bottom layer. Repeat with second and third layers, leaving enough of the mousse to spread on sides. Make sure layers are vertical; trim away any bulges with a serrated knife. Spread remaining mousse on sides of cake. Chill 30 minutes.

Pour half of warmed glaze over center of cake; spread towards edges and down sides. Cover sides of cake with remaining glaze. Chill before serving.

Caramel Apple Tartlets with Caramel Cages

The Range, Jackson, Wyoming

Tart Dough:

1 cup flour
1-1/2 teaspoons brown sugar
Pinch salt
2 ounces butter, chilled, cut in pieces
1 egg yolk
1/2 teaspoon vanilla
Ice water
1 egg white, lightly whipped

Combine dry ingredients in bowl of food processor; pulse to mix. Add butter, cutting into bits and pulsing until mixture resembles bread crumbs. With processor on, add egg yolk and vanilla. Add about 1-1/2 tablespoons ice water until dough begins to ball up when you pulse it. Stop machine when dough forms one large ball. Remove dough, wrap in plastic, refrigerate 1 hour.

Preheat oven to 350 degrees. Remove dough from refrigerator; let rest for 10 minutes. Cut into 6 pieces. On floured surface, roll out 1 piece to about 6" round. Gently place in tart tin and press into form. Line shells with paper or foil; weight with beans or rice. Put shells on a cookie sheet and bake for 10 minutes; rotate pan halfway through. Remove shells from oven; remove paper and beans. Prick shells with a fork and return to oven for 5 minutes. Remove shells from oven; brush inside of shells with egg whites. Cool on racks; refrigerate.

Caramel Apples:

1 cup heavy cream
1 ounce butter
1/4 cup light corn syrup
1/2 cup sugar
Pinch cream of tartar
1 tablespoon vanilla
3 to 4 large apples

In a quart saucepan, heat cream and butter to just below simmer. Combine syrup, sugar, and cream of tartar; microwave on high until mixture begins to bubble vigorously. Continue to cook, checking often. When a medium amber, remove from microwave. Sugar will continue to cook and darken.

Remove cream mixture from stove and add sugar mixture in a thin stream, stirring with a wooden spoon. (Be careful—much sputtering and steaming will occur!) When all sugar is added, check for any lumps of caramel; if necessary, return to stove over medium-low heat and stir until smooth. Cool mixture to room temperature and add vanilla.

Cut each apple into 8 wedges; core. In large bowl, coat apple wedges with half the caramel sauce. Divide remaining caramel sauce between pastry shells. With a slotted spoon, remove two wedges at a time and stand them up in the caramel in the shells. Form a "blossom" of 6 or 8 wedges in each

shell. As the caramel in the base of each shell cools, it will anchor the wedges. Refrigerate.

Caramel Cages:
1/4 cup light corn syrup
1/2 cup sugar
Pinch cream of tartar

Referring to previous recipe, repeat microwaving instructions.

Locate up to six small bowls, cups, etc. Lightly spray insides (or outsides) with vegetable oil spray. With a fork, dip into caramel and "lace" across the form, back and forth, to form a lattice. Cool and gently remove to a piece of parchment paper.

To assemble: Form a small pool of caramel/apple sauce on dessert plate. Place tartlet in the middle. Gently place a small scoop of ice cream in apple blossom. Cover with inverted caramel cage. Voila!

Pumpkin Cheesecake

La Comida, Cody, Wyoming

Mountain bikers and shoppers alike take refuge from the dry heat of Cody on the porch of La Comida, where they drink Dos Equis and contemplate such luscious dishes as blue corn tortillas with spinach and cheese or a Mexican praline tostada with vanilla ice cream.

Crust:

2 cups graham-cracker crumbs
2 tablespoons sugar
1/2 cup butter, melted

Preheat oven to 350 degrees. Combine crust ingredients and blend well with fingers. Press mixture evenly over bottom and 1 inch or so up sides of 9-1/2" springform pan. Bake crust for about 15 minutes. Let cool on rack.

Filling:

1 cup pumpkin puree
3/4 cup sugar
1/2 cup Amaretto
36 ounces cream cheese, softened
1/4 cup whipping cream
6 eggs
1/4 teaspoon nutmeg
1/4 teaspoon allspice
1/2 teaspoon cinnamon
1/8 teaspoon ground cloves

Decrease oven temperature to 275 degrees. To make filling, beat ingredients just until smooth, about 1 minute. Pour filling into crust, place pan in a waterbath, and bake in center of oven for 3 hours. Turn oven off, crack oven door open, and leave cheesecake in oven for another hour. Refrigerate 6 hours before cutting.

Right: La Comida Pumpkin Cheesecake

Chocolate-Strawberry-Banana Bandana Bundles on a Chocolate Wagon Wheel

Bundles:

1 teaspoon butter
1 banana, cut in half lengthwise and
    thinly sliced
4 ounces strawberries, sliced
1 tablespoon brown sugar
1 sheet puff pastry
2 ounces highest-quality semisweet
    chocolate bar, coarsely chopped

Preheat oven to 375 degrees. Lightly grease a baking sheet. Melt butter in sauté pan, then add bananas and strawberries, sautéing gently until soft. Turn up heat and add brown sugar; cook until sugar has melted, then cook a couple of minutes more, stirring gently. Cool.

Roll out puff pastry on a floured surface to an 11 x 11" square. Cut in half, then cut two 1/4" strips off the end of each pastry rectangle. Cut each rectangle in half. Divide chocolate among pastry pieces. Divide fruit evenly, mounding atop chocolate. Draw up corners of pastry and "tie" them together with a pastry strip. Remove to baking sheet and bake for about 35 minutes until golden brown.

Chocolate Sauce:

1/2 cup semisweet chocolate chips
2 tablespoons butter
Pinch of salt
1/4 cup half-and-half
1/4 teaspoon vanilla

Melt chocolate chips and butter in saucepan over low heat. Add salt, whisk in half-and-half until smooth, then stir in vanilla. Let cool slightly. Pour into a squeeze bottle.

Squeeze warm sauce onto 6 plates: draw a circle along each outer edge, then draw lines to make spokes of a wheel. Place a bundle in the center of each wheel. Sprinkle powdered sugar over the top and serve immediately.

Buffalo Bill Cody's
Red, White, and Blue Berry Shortcake

Buffalo Bill founded the town of Cody, and no holiday is more fun here than the Fourth of July, when the professional rodeo comes to town.

Strawberries:

3 cups strawberries, hulled and sliced
3 tablespoons sugar, or to taste

To prepare the "red": Combine strawberries and sugar in a bowl. Mash lightly with a fork. Cover and chill, stirring occasionally, for 1 hour.

Shortcakes:

2 cups flour
1 tablespoon baking powder
3/4 teaspoon salt
3 tablespoons sugar
4 ounces pure almond paste, crumbled
4 tablespoons butter, chilled and cut into pieces
1 cup buttermilk, more for the glaze

To make the almond shortcakes, preheat oven to 400 degrees. Lightly grease a baking sheet. In a large bowl, whisk the flour, baking powder, salt, and sugar. Cut in the butter and almond paste with a pastry knife or fingertips until mixture resembles coarse crumbs. Gently stir in buttermilk until just combined with flour mixture. Spoon the dough onto the prepared baking sheet in 6 equal mounds. Sprinkle a heaping tablespoon of sliced almonds onto each shortcake and gently press into batter. Bake until light brown, about 20 to 25 minutes. Let rest for 1 minute and then cool slightly on wire rack. Slice open warm shortcakes horizontally with a serrated knife.

(cont'd)

Blueberry Sauce:

3 cups (about 1 pound) blueberries, rinsed and patted dry, plus a few extra blueberries for garnish
2 tablespoons sugar, or to taste
2 teaspoons water

To make the "blue": In medium saucepan, combine 2 cups of blueberries, sugar, and water. Cook uncovered over medium heat for 6 to 7 minutes until very soft and juicy, stirring frequently. Stir in remaining cup of blueberries. Refrigerate or serve warm, if desired.

Whipped Cream:

1-1/2 cups whipping cream, chilled
2 tablespoons powdered sugar
1 teaspoon vanilla

To make the "white": In a chilled bowl, beat the heavy cream until it just holds soft peaks. Beat in the powdered sugar and vanilla, and beat the mixture until it holds stiff peaks.

To assemble: Place bottom half of each shortcake on a serving plate. Spoon over about 1/4 cup of blueberry sauce, 1/4 cup strawberries, and a few dollops of cream. Top with other half of the shortcake. Spoon on more blueberries and strawberries; add another dollop of cream. Garnish with a whole strawberry and/or blueberries, if desired.

Right: Buffalo Bill Cody's Red, White, and Blue Berry Shortcake

Green Apple Sorbet and Vanilla Bean Ice Cream with Caramel Sauce

Log Haven Restaurant, Salt Lake City, Utah

The Log Haven Restaurant lies near the Wasatch wilderness in a 1920s log mansion, where Chef David Jones offers award-winning cuisine and superlative desserts: a macadamia-nut tart, chocolate bread pudding, and mango sorbet.

Green Apple Sorbet:

**11 apples, peeled and cored
(Granny Smith does well)
37 ounces apple juice
9 ounces sugar
Dash of lemon juice**

Puree ingredients together; strain. Freeze according to instructions for your ice-cream maker.

Vanilla Bean Ice Cream:

**42 ounces milk
14 ounces cream (11 cups)
2 cups sugar
4 vanilla beans
1/2 ounce vanilla
11 egg yolks**

Combine milk, cream, 1 cup sugar, and vanilla beans in a heavy saucepan and bring to a boil. Remove from heat and let sit for 15 minutes. Add remaining half of the sugar and the egg yolks; stir over medium heat until it reaches the ribbon stage (mixture will fall from spoon in a continuous ribbon). Place yolks in a double boiler over water bath and simmer 4 to 5 minutes. Combine. Chill, then freeze.

Caramel Sauce:

**1/3 cup sugar
1/3 cup water
1 tablespoon butter
1 tablespoon heavy cream**

Spread sugar evenly in a skillet over medium heat and stir constantly until sugar turns amber in color. Add water and cook until caramel has dissolved. Finish by stirring in cream and butter.

Bartlett Pear Tarte Tatin with Vanilla Sauce

Skyline Guest Ranch, Telluride, Colorado

Crust:

3 cups plus 1-1/2 teaspoons all-purpose flour
1 cup butter, softened
7-1/2 tablespoons cold water

Filling:

1-3/4 pounds Bartlett pears, peeled and cored
2 cups sugar
1 tablespoon lemon juice
1 tablespoon cinnamon
1/4 cup butter, cut into cubes

Combine flour and butter in a food processor and pulse just until the butter is incorporated. Add cold water and pulse until dough comes together in a ball. Gather and let rest for 1 hour. Meanwhile, using a heavy 10" or 12" sauté pan with an ovenproof handle, layer 1 cup of sugar evenly on the bottom of the pan. Layer pears evenly, sprinkle with lemon juice and cinnamon, dot with butter.

Preheat oven to 350 degrees. Roll pie dough out to 1/4" thickness. Cover pears with the crust and tuck edges under the fruit. Heat skillet on the stovetop on high until sugar is just melted. Place in oven and bake about 30 to 40 minutes until crust is golden brown and sugar is caramelized. Allow to cool slightly, then slip out onto large serving plate or dish.

Vanilla Sauce:

1 quart heavy cream
2 cups powdered sugar
1 ounce cornstarch
2 tablespoons vanilla

Heat cream, sugar, and cornstarch. Bring to a boil until the mixture has thickened but still has a saucelike consistency. Add vanilla; strain and cool.

Warm Chocolate Soufflé
with Chocolate Glaze and Mascarpone Cream
The Snake River Grill, Jackson, Wyoming

The Snake River Grill serves fresh fish, free-range veal and chicken, indigenous game, organic produce, and pizzas from a wood-burning oven. This dessert is from pastry chef Deno Marcum.

Soufflé:

1-1/4 sticks unsalted butter

6 ounces bittersweet or semisweet chocolate, chopped into small pieces

4 egg yolks

1/3 cup plus 1 tablespoon sugar

4 egg whites

2 teaspoons lemon juice

Preheat oven to 350 degrees. Butter and dust eight 6-ounce ramekins with sugar. Over a bath of simmering water, melt butter and chocolate. Beat egg yolks and 1/3 cup sugar to the "ribbon stage" (when mixture falls from beaters in a continuous ribbon), then mix into chocolate mixture. Whip egg whites, 1 tablespoon sugar, and lemon juice so it holds very soft peaks. Fold gently into the chocolate-yolk mixture. Divide mixture among ramekins.

Bake for 16 to 30 minutes until a toothpick inserted in the middle comes out clean. Allow to rest for 5 minutes. Invert the soufflés and allow to cool another 5 minutes.

1-1/4 sticks unsalted butter

6 ounces bittersweet or semisweet
  chocolate

1 tablespoon light corn syrup

Combine ingredients in double boiler or metal bowl placed over a pan of simmering water and melt, whisking occasionally until smooth.

Mascarpone Cream:

1 cup heavy cream

1 tablespoon sugar

5 ounces mascarpone cheese, stirred
  until soft

Combine ingredients in a bowl. Using the whisk attachment of a mixer, slowly combine ingredients and continue stirring until cream begins to "trace" (hold the lines made by the whisk). Increase speed and continue to whisk until mixture is very stiff.

To assemble: Unmold the soufflés and place each one in the center of a plate. Pour about 2 ounces of glaze over each, garnish with mascarpone cream, and serve immediately.

Resource Directory

Noteworthy Restaurants and Inns of the Northern Rockies

The Gallatin Gateway Inn
Highway 191
P.O. Box 376
Gallatin Gateway, Montana 59730
406-763-4672

La Comida
1385 Sheridan Avenue
Cody, Wyoming 82414
307-587-9556

Log Haven
Millcreek Canyon
P.O. Box 9154
Salt Lake City, Utah 84109
801-272-8255

Maxwell's
937 Sheridan Avenue
Cody, Wyoming 82414
307-527-7749

The Park Cafe
Highway 89
St. Mary, Montana 59417
406-732-4482

The Range
225 North Cache Drive
Jackson, Wyoming 83001
307-733-5481

Skyline Guest Ranch
P.O. Box 67
Telluride, Colorado 81435
970-728-3757

The Snake River Grill
84 East Broadway
Jackson, Wyoming 83001
307-733-0557

Spanish Peaks Brewing Company
120 North 19th Avenue
P.O. Box 3644
Bozeman, Montana 59772
406-585-2296

The Sun Valley Lodge Dining Room
Sun Valley Resort
Sun Valley, Idaho 83353
208-622-4111
800-786-8259

Index